MY FIRST LOOK AT PLANETS

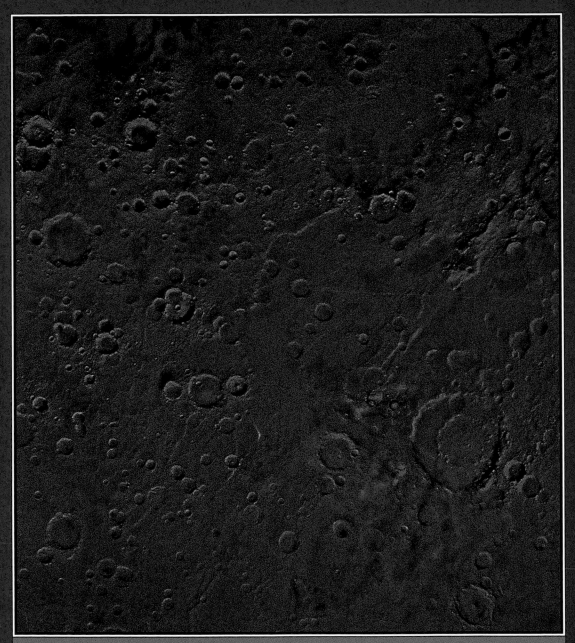

THE SURFACE OF MARS IS RED AND ROUGH

Mars

TERESA WIMMER

CREATIVE EDUCATION

Published by Creative Education

P.O. Box 227, Mankato, Minnesota 56002

Creative Education is an imprint of The Creative Company

Designed by Rita Marshall

Photographs by Getty Images (Iconica, Riser), Tom Stack & Associates (ESA, JPL, NASA,

Inga Spence, TASDO, USGS)

Copyright © 2008 Creative Education

Printed in the United States of America

Library of Congress Cataloging-in-Publication Data

Wimmer, Teresa, 1975- Mars / by Teresa Wimmer.

p. cm. — (My first look at planets)

Includes index.

ISBN-13: 978-1-58341-518-4

1. Mars (Planet)—Juvenile literature. I. Title.

QB641.W56 2007   523.43—dc22   2006018248

First edition 9 8 7 6 5 4 3 2 1

Mars

RED BALL

At night, people can look up in the sky and see the **planet** Mars. It looks like a bright red ball in the dark sky. Many people call Mars the "red planet."

Mars is part of the **solar system**. Besides Mars, there are seven other planets. All of the planets move in an **orbit** around the sun. Mars is the fourth planet from the sun.

THE SUN LIGHTS HALF OF MARS AT A TIME

Like Earth, Mars is made of rock. It has tall mountains and deep ditches called valleys. There is ice at the top and bottom of Mars.

DRY AND SANDY

Mars is a very dry place. It has no lakes, rivers, or streams. Mars has hot mountains called volcanoes. There are many hills made of red sand. Sometimes strong winds blow across Mars. They send the sand flying.

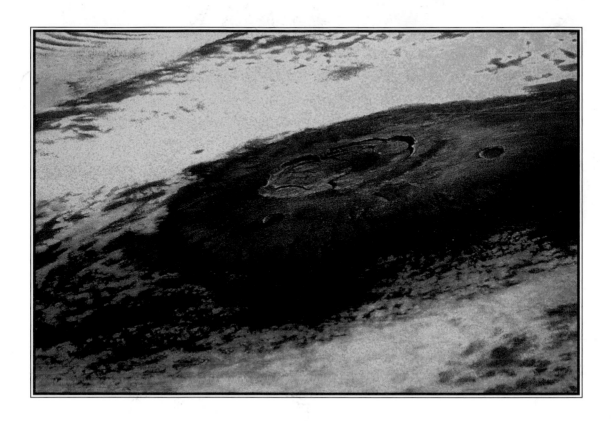

Mars has the tallest volcano
in the solar system. Its
name is Olympus Mons.

Sometimes the winds calm down. Then the sun comes out. But the air still stays very cold. Even in the summer it does not get above 0 °F (–18 °C).

Mars has a winter **season**, too. Winter is even colder than summer. Sometimes there is frost on the ground. But there is never any snow. You could not build a snowman on Mars!

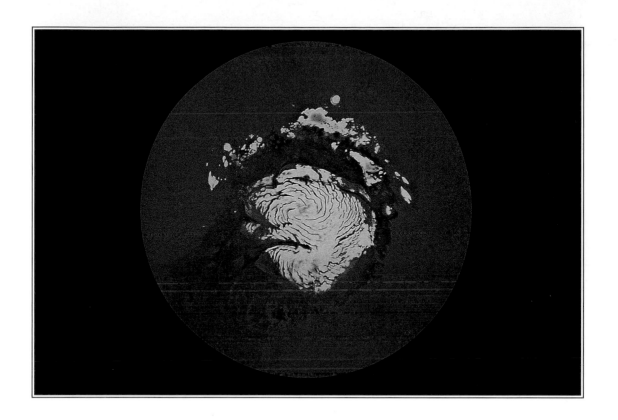

Mars looks red

because of a metal called

iron in its air and dirt.

MOONS OF MARS

Mars has two moons. The moons are named Phobos (*FOE-bus*) and Deimos (*DEE-mohs*). They move in an orbit around Mars. Both moons are small and rocky. They look like potatoes in the sky.

Phobos orbits close to Mars. It dashes around Mars three times a day. Phobos is moving closer and closer to Mars. One day, it might even crash into Mars!

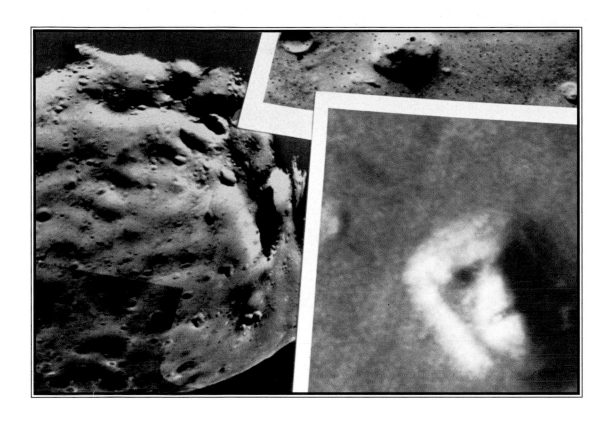

Pictures from probes show
a special hill on Mars. It
is shaped like a face!

More to Learn

Many people want to learn more about Mars. They send probes there. The probes have special cameras on them. The cameras take pictures of Mars.

The pictures show lines called channels in Mars's ground. Some people think Mars had rivers a long time ago. The rivers might have made the channels. Then the rivers dried up.

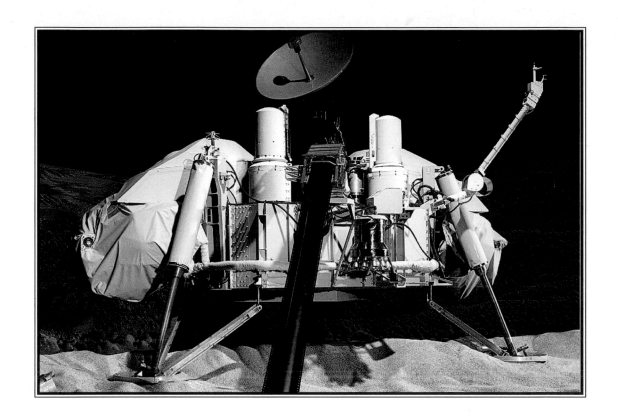

Sometimes small rocks fall
off Mars. People on Earth
have found some of the rocks.

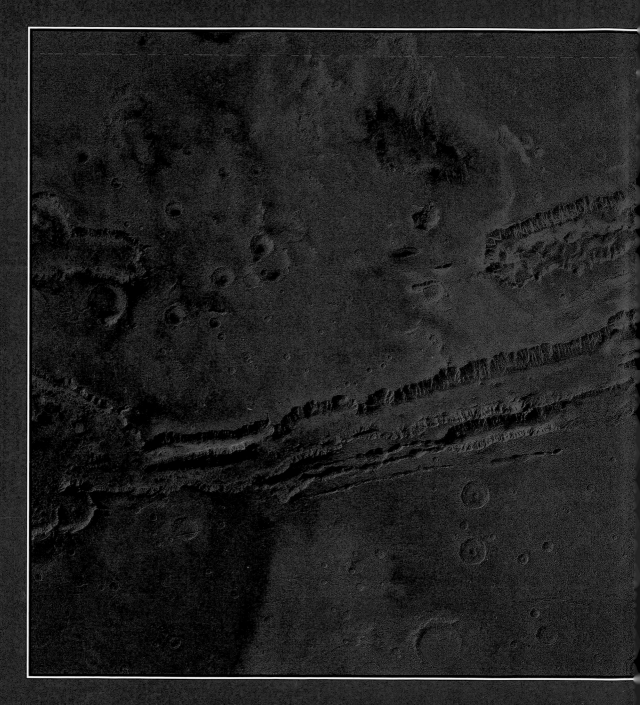

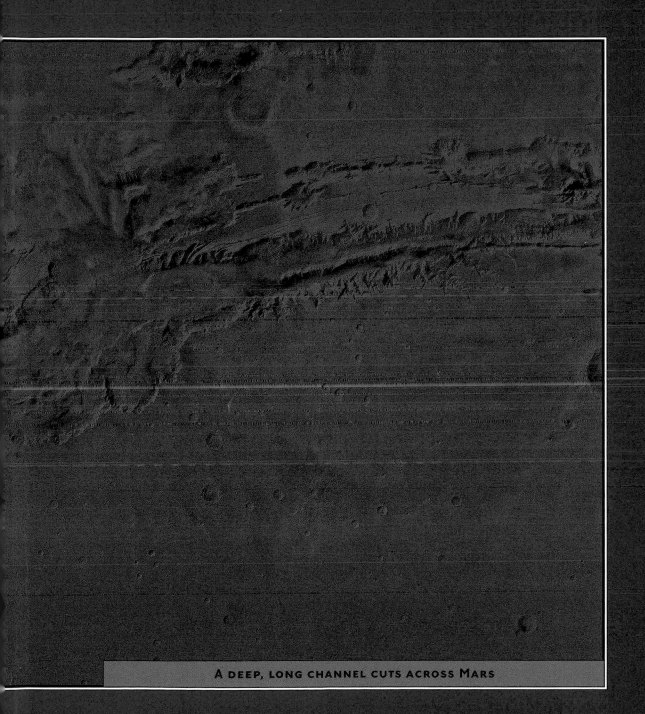

A deep, long channel cuts across Mars

The pictures do not show any people, animals, or plants living on Mars. Mars has no water to drink. It has almost no fresh air to breathe.

Someday, people might be able to fly a spaceship to Mars. They would have to bring along fresh air and water. Then they could stay for a while!

PROBES SEND PICTURES TO BIG RECEIVERS ON EARTH

Hands-on: Make a Planet Mars

Mars is a pretty, red planet. You can make your very own Mars and watch it spin!

What You Need

A small Styrofoam ball

A piece of yarn about eight
   inches (20 cm) long

A red marker

A pen

Glue

What You Do

1. Color the Styrofoam ball red.
2. Draw a few pen lines on the ball for channels.
3. Glue one end of the yarn to the top of the ball.
4. Now you have your own planet Mars. Hold on to the top of the yarn. Make Mars spin!

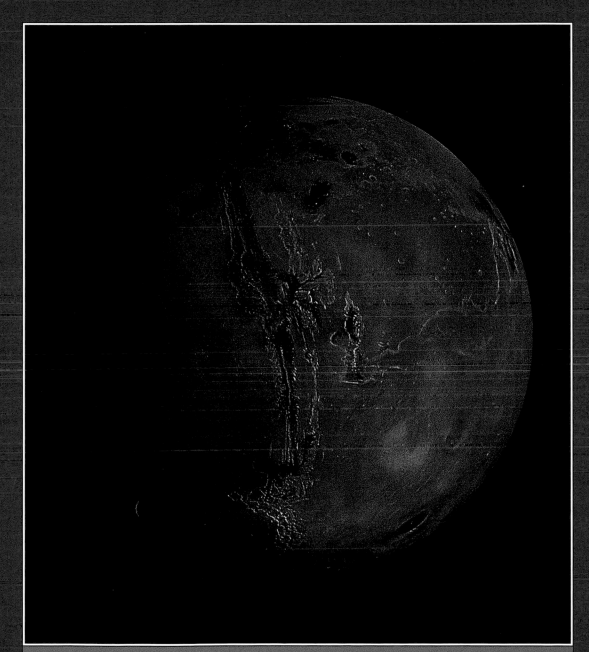

MARS DOES NOT LOOK LIKE ANY OTHER PLANET

Index

Words to Know

orbit—the path a planet takes around the sun or a moon takes around a planet

planet—a round object that moves around the sun

probes—special machines that fly around or land on a planet or a moon

season—different times of year; the seasons are winter, spring, summer, and fall

solar system—the sun, the planets, and their moons

Read More

Chrismer, Melanie. *Mars.* New York: Scholastic, 2005.

Rudy, Lisa Jo. *Planets!* New York: HarperCollins, 2005.

Vogt, Gregory. *Solar System.* New York: Scholastic, 2001.

Explore the Web

Enchanted Learning: Mars http://www.zoomschool.com/subjects/astronomy/
planets/mars

Funschool: Space http://funschool.kaboose.com/globe-rider/space/
index.html?trnstl=1

StarChild: The Planet Mars http://starchild.gsfc.nasa.gov/docs/StarChild/
solar_system_level1/mars.html